WHEN TALKING GETS TOUGH

HOW TO HAVE IMPORTANT CONVERSATIONS

WHEN TALKING GETS TOUGH

HOW TO HAVE IMPORTANT CONVERSATIONS

Scott T. Brown

Church &
Family Life

Wake Forest, NC

Church & Family Life
220 South White St., Wake Forest, NC 27587
www.churchandfamilylife.com

ISBN: 978-1-62418-067-5

CONTENTS

INTRODUCTION

Death and life are in the power of the tongue, and those who love it will eat its fruit. (Prov. 18:21)

One of the most important things you will ever do is learn to talk—and listen. This is especially vital when *controversial subjects*, *pivotal relationships*, *strong opinions*, and *important outcomes* are at play.

This book is designed to help you have profitable conversations amid such challenges.

Sound discourse is a discipline that must be learned. It requires humble restraint under the authority of biblical commands and practices.

This flies in the face of our age which idolizes self-expression and encourages us to "Be true to yourself," "Let it all hang out," and "Speak your truth." Such advice is a broad path that leads to ruin.

With all that's at stake, we must wisely equip ourselves for the tough conversations that are inevitable with parents, spouses, children, friends, and bosses.

What is there to disagree about? Plenty! Especially because we are people who change as time goes on.

- Convictions change over time
- Lifestyle preferences change
- Children change and often begin to think differently than their parents
- Friends change
- Couples change

By definition, the very process of growing involves change. This should be expected. We will change as we grow.

Yet managing seasons of change can be difficult. When we are changing, we are often vulnerable to extreme opinions. These opinions may cause unnecessary disruptions in our relationships.

When you are engaging in such heavyweight matters, it is important that you know how to talk.

Huge consequences hang in the balance. How we talk will determine the direction of our relationships, for:

- Talking is how we work through disagreements
- Talking is how we express strong opinions
- Talking is how we share our concerns
- Talking is how we make plans
- Talking is how we change the course of our lives

Getting a handle on our speech is therefore an imperative.

THE POWER OF THE TONGUE

You must stay at the helm of your tongue, for it acts as a "rudder," James explains (James 3:4). Your tongue is always taking you somewhere—and without careful guidance, it will lead you to shipwreck.

The tongue is also "a fire" that can easily burn relationships to the ground (James 3:5-6).

Left in our sinful state, our mouths will spew forth "deadly poison" (James 3:8; Matt. 15:19; Gal. 5:19-21).

As sobering as the bad news is, the good news is wonderful. The tongue can not only destroy, but it can also build up—for both "Death and life are in the power of the tongue" (Prov. 18:21).

Our words can thus be a "tree of life" (Prov. 15:4); full of "grace, seasoned with salt" (Col. 4:6); "like apples of gold in settings of silver" (Prov. 25:11); and a spring of "fresh water" (James 3:11).

TWO TRAPS

When it comes to speech, two extremes threaten our conversations.

The first threat comes from popular psychotherapy. The modern therapeutic culture encourages us to "Tell all." It goes like this: in order to be authentic and true to yourself, you are obligated to share all your inmost thoughts, feelings, and desires. Scripture condemns this crazy notion:

A fool vents all his feelings, but a wise man holds them back. (Prov. 29:11)

The heart of the righteous studies how to answer, but the mouth of the wicked pours forth evil. (Prov. 15:28)

We are fools if we speak every single thought that enters our minds! A wise man will carefully measure his words.

The second threat is also dangerous—silence. This is when we consciously withdraw into self-absorbed protection when words should be spoken.

This can be caused by pride. It happens when we want to avoid having our ideas challenged: "A man who isolates himself seeks his own desire; he rages against all wise judgment" (Prov. 18:1).

It can also be caused by the fear of man, which "is a snare" (Prov. 29:25).

Retreating into one's turtle shell when words are called for is no more acceptable than blurting out everything on your mind. This is why learning how to talk is so important.

As we engage in hard conversations, our tongues should pour forth the water of life rather than the venom of death. My hope is to give you faithful truths so you might bring such life with your tongue.

Scott Brown
Wake Forest, NC
August 2023

THE PREEMINENT MOTIVE

Why do you want to learn to talk well? Is it for selfish motives or for the glory of Christ?

Many crave self-help techniques to make them better communicators. And there are certainly nifty tips to improve your speech. For example, you can learn to talk:

- To have smoother relationships
- To be more successful
- So that you can get your way more often
- So that people will flatter you as a good communicator
- So that people will regard you as discerning
- For your own self-aggrandizement

Smooth talk can get you all of these outcomes.

But that's not the goal of this book. This book is not written to teach clever stratagems of speech. It is written for those who earnestly desire, in their heart of hearts, to please God with their words.

As Christians, we should yearn to glorify God in our bodies (1 Cor. 6:20), presenting our tongues and every part of ourselves as a "living sacrifice, holy, and acceptable to God" (Rom. 12:1). We should strive to bring "every thought into captivity to the obedience of Christ" (2 Cor. 10:5). The longing of our hearts should be this: "Let the words of my mouth and the meditation of my heart be acceptable in Your sight, O Lord, my strength and my Redeemer" (Ps. 19:14).

Paul Washer has well observed, "The believer's interests and affections need to be refined and redirected not merely from the bad to the good, but from the good to the most excellent."[1]

Simply put, the supreme motive for learning how to talk must be to become like Christ. That's it. Nothing more will do. There is no higher motive. We were created "that in all things He might have the preeminence" (Col. 1:18).

REGENERATION: THE STARTING POINT FOR SOUND SPEECH

To speak like Christ, we must be regenerated. This is the sole starting point. God-glorifying speech is a manifestation of true conversion. The believer brings down God's perfect gifts from heaven to earth. There is no other source. James writes:

> *Do not be deceived, my beloved brethren. Every good gift and every perfect gift is from above, and comes down from the Father of lights, with whom there is no variation or shadow of turning. Of His own will He brought us forth by the word of truth, that we might be a kind of firstfruits of His creatures. (James 1:16-18)*

---

1   Paul Washer, *The Preeminent Christ* (Grand Rapids: Reformation Heritage Books, 2023), p. 59.

God renovates our nature, and we become fruitful, James explains. When God saves a person, good gifts fall upon him, and that man becomes a "kind of firstfruits of His creatures" (James 1:18).

After stating this fact, James immediately explains one way it manifests—it shows itself in the way we talk: "So then, my beloved brethren, let every man be swift to hear, slow to speak, slow to wrath; for the wrath of man does not produce the righteousness of God" (James 1:19-20).

SANCTIFICATION: PUT OFF THE OLD MAN

Though regeneration is the starting point for right speech, sanctification must follow, as we still wrestle with leftovers from the old man (Rom. 7:23). James remarks, "Out of the same mouth proceed blessing and cursing. My brethren, these things ought not to be so" (James 3:19).

We must "no longer walk as" an unbeliever, affirms the Apostle Paul (Eph. 4:17). Instead, we are to "put off, concerning your former conduct, the old man which grows corrupt according to the deceitful lusts, and be renewed in the spirit of your mind, and that you put on the new man which was created according to God, in true righteousness and holiness" (Eph. 4:22-24).

Paul then adds this: "Let no corrupt word proceed out of your mouth, but what is good for necessary edification, that it may impart grace to the hearers" (Eph. 4:29).

OUR EVERY WORD AND MOTIVE WILL BE JUDGED

God hears all our words—be they corrupt or pure. And, in the end, our every word will be judged. Jesus said, "But I say to you that for every idle word men may speak, they will give account of it in the day of judgment" (Matt. 12:36).

We live before the face of God, plain and simple. This is the meaning of, "Coram Deo." There is no hiding our motives from Him, "You have set our iniquities before You, our secret sins in the light of Your countenance" (Ps. 90:8). Ambrose of Milan remarked:

> *If thou canst not hide thyself from the sun, which is God's minister of light, how impossible will it be to hide thyself from Him, Whose eyes are ten thousand times brighter than the sun!*[2]

At God's Final Judgment, secret sins will be revealed. Evil motives will be shown for all their wickedness. Manipulative speech will be unmasked. Lies will be laid bare. And every word driven by the desire to exalt ourselves will be fully exposed: "For God shall bring every work into judgment, with every secret thing, whether it be good, or whether it be evil" (Eccl. 12:14).

---

2   As quoted by Thomas Brooks, "The Privy Key of Heaven," *The Works of Thomas Brooks, Vol. II* (Edinburgh: James Nichol, 1866), p. 285.

WHAT OUR CHIEF MOTIVE SHOULD BE: BECOME LIKE CHRIST!

While we should desire to escape the consequences of our idle and selfish words, our chief motive to learn to talk well is to become like Jesus Christ—to hunger and thirst after righteousness and be fully conformed to His perfect image (Matt. 5:6; Rom. 8:29). This should be our deepest desire.

My prayer for this book is that Christ would be preeminent in our speech. Jesus spoke perfectly, and the people marveled at His words, saying, "No man ever spoke like this man!" (John 7:46). What a blessing it would be if the likeness of Jesus would become progressively manifested in all our conversations!

The most blessed speech comes when we are simultaneously before the face of man, and transformed by the countenance of our Lord Jesus Christ:

> But we all, with unveiled face, beholding as in a mirror the glory of the Lord, are being transformed into the same image from glory to glory, just as by the Spirit of the Lord. (2 Cor. 3:18)

Puritan Isaac Ambrose captured the beauty of this in his classic work, *Looking unto Jesus:*

> Oh! How should all hearts be taken with this Christ? Christians! Turn your eyes upon the Lord. "Look, and look again unto Jesus." Why stand ye gazing on the toys of this world, when such a Christ is offered to you in the gospel? Can the world die for you? Can the world reconcile you

to the Father? Can the world advance you to the kingdom of heaven? As Christ is all in all, so let him be the full and complete subject of our desire, and hope, and faith, and love, and joy; let Him be in your thoughts the first in the morning, and the last at night.[3]

Let this be our motive for learning how to talk.

---

3   Isaac Ambrose, *Looking unto Jesus: A View of the Everlasting Gospel* (Harrisonburg, VA: Sprinkle Publications, 1986), p. 694.

SCRIPTURE IS SUFFICIENT TO TEACH US

THE WORD OF GOD IS EVERYTHING YOU NEED

God teaches us how to talk. In His Word, He has given us all we need to govern our speech.

The doctrine of the sufficiency of Scripture states that God has given us everything necessary for life and godliness. What a comfort it is to know that the answers we are looking for are to be found in the Bible!

While the world desperately searches for good communication skills, the search for the Christian is over. We have God's perfect Word:

All Scripture is given by inspiration of God, and is profitable for doctrine, for reproof, for correction, for instruction in righteousness, that the man of God may be complete, thoroughly equipped for every good work. (2 Tim. 3:16-17)

The 1689 London Baptist Confession of Faith describes the sufficiency of Scripture this way:

The Holy Scripture is the only sufficient, certain, and infallible rule of all saving knowledge, faith, and obedience. (LBC 1.1)

The whole counsel of God concerning all things necessary for His own glory, man's salvation, faith and life, is either expressly set down or necessarily contained in the Holy Scripture: unto which nothing at any time is to be added, whether by new revelation of the Spirit, or traditions of men. (LBC 1.6)

David gives this poignant assurance:

The law of the LORD is perfect, converting the soul; the testimony of the LORD is sure, making wise the simple; the statutes of the LORD are right, rejoicing the heart; the commandment of the LORD is pure, enlightening the eyes; . . . Moreover by them Your servant is warned, and in keeping them there is great reward. (Ps. 19:7-8, 11)

The fact that we have this life-giving roadmap for our speech is a great blessing. Yet most of us have well-worn patterns of communication in direct odds with it. These patterns have been shaped by sin, by family culture, and by the world, the flesh, and the devil over many years. So to speak as we ought, these patterns must be broken.

This will only happen through the illumination of the Word of God, the transforming power of the Holy Spirit, and active obedience.

LEARNING HOW TO TALK IS THE FRUIT OF LEARNING HOW TO LOVE

What makes us well-equipped to speak as we should in hard conversations is not eloquent speech or a polished vocabulary—but Christian love. This is the heart of the matter. Paul writes: "Though I speak with the tongues of men and of angels, but have not love, I have become sounding brass or a clanging cymbal" (1 Cor. 13:1).

To put the matter simply: proper speaking flows from the Second Greatest Commandment: "You shall love your neighbor as yourself" (Matt. 22:39).

Yet such love doesn't come naturally. Katherine Anne Porter rightly states, "Love must be learned, and learned again and again; there is no end to it. Hate needs no instruction, but waits only to be provoked."[1]

We must learn the path of love for others in our speech. But before we examine this path, let us consider harmful ways of conversing that flow from loving ourselves.

---

1   Katherine Anne Porter, "The Necessary Enemy," *The Collected Essays and Occasional Writings of Katherine Anne Porter* (New York: Delacorte Press, 1970), p. 184.

NINETEEN HARMFUL PATTERNS OF COMMUNICATION

LANDMINES THAT BLOW UP CONVERSATIONS

One of the difficulties with having important and meaningful conversations is that there is always something lurking under the surface. Significant conversations are like icebergs—only the tip is showing. Underneath are assumptions, feelings, experiences, and motives.

Some of these underlying thoughts and motives are toxic. These are the snakes, bats, and scorpions of our inner world. They surface through habits of speech and volatile emotions. They are dark impulses within.

Their shape is ugly—yet familiar. If you want to sin and sabotage a good conversation, here are nineteen ways to do it:

1. **Interrupt** the other person mid-sentence
2. Abruptly **contradict** them
3. **Presume you understand** what they're saying
4. **Focus on winning**
5. **Make threats**

6. **Name call** rather than address the issues raised
7. **Discredit** rather than evaluate differences of opinion
8. **Label and objectify** rather than deal with real concerns
9. **Blame** them or others rather than take personal responsibility
10. Give them the **"cold shoulder"**
11. Give them the **"silent treatment"**
12. **Act with aggression**
13. **Withdraw in sullenness**
14. **Hurl insults**
15. **Exaggerate** the issues
16. **Take cheap shots**
17. **Overshare** instead of speaking with discretion
18. **Walk out** in the middle of the conversation
19. Selfishly **lie**

Is this how you want to talk? Invariably, at the bottom of these speech patterns is some underlying sin: pride, self-centeredness, self-aggrandizement, manipulation, lack of self-control, hatred, railing, misrepresentation, narcissism, etc.

Take a careful inventory of your conversations. If you have been manifesting any of these bad traits, you are in trouble.

Here is an exercise: Make a copy of these toxic speech habits and carry them with you. When you are about to get into a difficult conversation, review the list. Ask the Lord to keep you from falling into these traps.

But don't stop there. Pursue good patterns! Focus on the best and most biblical ways of communicating.

Learning how to speak begins as we "look, and look again unto Jesus."

Following are thirteen practical behaviors to guide your speech. This is a biblical roadmap for how to successfully engage in difficult, emotionally charged, and pivotal conversations.

THIRTEEN BEHAVIORS TO SWEETEN DIFFICULT CONVERSATIONS

I. PREPARE YOUR HEART (MATT. 12:34-37)

As we consider walking into a difficult conversation, we must carefully prepare our hearts. This is the critical first step before moving forward.

Just what are our motivations in having this hard talk? What's percolating inside? Are you uptight? Are you angry? Are you bitter? Are you discouraged? Are you digesting the tender morsels of slander? Are you being driven by genuine love for the other person, or are you fueled by prideful self-interest?

Know that your heart will always determine your speech. Your motives will be reflected in what you say. "For out of the abundance of the heart the mouth speaks. A good man out of the good treasure of his heart brings forth good things, and an evil man out of the evil treasure brings forth evil things" (Matt. 12:34-35). This is why we are admonished: "Keep your heart with all diligence, for out of it spring the issues of life" (Prov. 4:23).

Your heart must thus be corralled and right with God before you open your mouth.

Paul admonishes:

Let nothing be done through selfish ambition or conceit, but in lowliness of mind let each esteem others better than himself. Let each of you look out not only for his own interests, but also for the interests of others. Let this mind be in you which was also in Christ Jesus. (Phil. 2:3-5)

Rooted and Grounded in Love

God calls us to be "rooted and grounded in love" (Eph. 3:17), to "walk in love, as Christ also has loved us and given Himself for us" (Eph. 5:2), and to "[speak] the truth in love" (Eph. 4:15).

This love is not intangible sentiment; it should color every corner of our hearts and directly shape how we exchange words with others:

Love suffers long and is kind; love does not envy; love does not parade itself, is not puffed up; does not behave rudely, does not seek its own, is not provoked, thinks no evil; does not rejoice in iniquity, but rejoices in the truth; bears all things, believes all things, hopes all things, endures all things. Love never fails. (1 Cor. 13:4-8)

Preparing one's heart begins with love. And once love becomes your guiding principle, it will clarify ten thousand other details.

Love does not harbor petty offenses. So if you're about to blow your stack over some major or even minor infraction, stop and change course. This is the type of "hard conversation" that shouldn't happen.

Both Solomon and Peter speak to this: "The discretion of a man makes him slow to anger, and his glory is to overlook a transgression" (Prov. 19:11); "And above all things have fervent love for one another, for 'love will cover a multitude of sins'" (1 Pet. 4:8).

Nor does love think the worst of others. In thinking the worst, we often inject motives where they do not exist. Love does not think the worst; it thinks the best instead. Love "thinks no evil" (1 Cor. 13:5). So if you're building a case against someone in your heart without just cause, you should cease and desist.

Love is forbearing and forgiving. Paul writes to the Colossians:

Therefore, as the elect of God, holy and beloved, put on tender mercies, kindness, humility, meekness, longsuffering; bearing with one another, and forgiving one another, if anyone has a complaint against another; even as Christ forgave you, so you also must do. (Col. 3:12-13)

Christ freely forgave, and so must you. You should not hold grudges and pour forth venom when wronged. Rather than be quick to retort when you're slighted, be longsuffering.

When Love Requires Confrontation

There are times, however, when love requires confrontation. Solomon makes this clear: "Open rebuke is better than love carefully concealed. Faithful are the wounds of a friend" (Prov. 27:5-6).

Moses declared that a needed rebuke is an act of love. And there are times when to neglect that needed rebuke is an act of hatred (Lev. 19:17-18). Silence is often a way we are hating our brother.

Paul also called the Thessalonian church to "warn those who are unruly" (1 Thess. 5:14-15).

The Lord Jesus Himself told His disciples: "if your brother sins against you, go and tell him his fault between you and him alone. If he hears you, you have gained your brother" (Matt. 18:15).

Yet even when love calls for confrontation, it also governs how it should be carried out. Love demands a careful "heart examination" and thoughtful preparation. Your heart and "bedside manner" matter; you're not free to confront another person in any old way.

A Seven-Point Heart Check

Paul prescribes a seven-point heart check that must be followed when pursuing confrontation. These questions will help you hold fast to God's blueprint for conversations. They will keep you on course and tell you if you're headed for trouble.

Brethren, if a man is overtaken in any trespass, you who are spiritual restore such a one in a spirit of gentleness, considering yourself lest you also be tempted. Bear one another's burdens, and so fulfill the law of Christ. For if anyone thinks himself to be something, when he is nothing, he deceives himself. (Gal. 6:1-3)

Checkpoint One: Has your brother been "overtaken in any trespass" (Gal. 6:1)?

A trespass is not an eccentric quirk. It is not a misstep or an accident. It is not an annoying idiosyncrasy. These are not grounds to confront your brother.

A trespass is a fall. It is "a lapse or deviation from truth and uprightness; a sin, misdeed."[1] It may or may not be premeditated. It may be unintentional (there are unintentional sins). The whole armor of God was not in place. Perhaps your brother was particularly vulnerable because of underlying sins.

If you are married, and have a grievance against your spouse, make sure you are dealing with real sins. Make sure you are evaluating your spouse's actions against this standard. Only move forward with correction if they have truly trespassed.

Checkpoint Two: Are you spiritually-minded or earthly-minded (Gal. 6:1)?

Is your mind "filled with the knowledge of His will in all wisdom and spiritual understanding" (Col. 1:9), or is it carnal in nature? You must get to the bottom of this before proceeding.

In the text immediately preceding this seven-pronged test, Paul explains what being spiritually minded looks like:

> But the fruit of the Spirit is love, joy, peace, longsuffering, kindness, goodness, faithfulness, gentleness, self-control. Against such there is no law. And those who are Christ's

---

1   *paraptōma* (G3900 in *Strong's*), definition in *Thayer's Greek Lexicon* (1896).

*have crucified the flesh with its passions and desires. If
we live in the Spirit, let us also walk in the Spirit. Let us
not become conceited, provoking one another, envying one
another. (Gal. 5:22-26)*

Being Spirit-driven rather than flesh-driven when you confront
someone is crucial, "for to be carnally minded is death, but to be
spiritually minded is life and peace" (Rom. 8:6)—so be sure to
get this right before you have a hard conversation!

Checkpoint Three: Are you pursuing the right objective—to "restore such a one" (Gal. 6:1)?

The word "restore" speaks of putting a dislocated limb back in
place. The word is also used of fishermen mending their nets.[2]
A process of repair is implied in this metaphor. As you weigh
your words, be aware that your speech will always take you in
a particular direction, so make sure your words take you to
the right destination. When dealing with a brother "overtaken
in any trespass" (Gal. 6:1), drive toward restoration, and don't
say anything that would divert you from this end. Do not allow
emotions to cloud your vision. Don't let offenses get in the way
of this primary objective.

---

2   On putting back a dislocated limb, see: John MacArthur, *Galatians: The
    MacArthur New Testament Commentary* (Chicago: Moody Publisher, 1987), p.
    179. On mending nets, see: William Hendriksen, *Galatians and Ephesians: New
    Testament Commentary by William Hendriksen* (Grand Rapids, Baker Book
    House, 1979), p. 232.

Checkpoint Four: Are you operating in a "spirit of gentleness"
(Gal. 6:1)?

Gentleness is a fruit of the Spirit (Gal. 5:23) that is required of
Christians when they bring correction:

> *And a servant of the Lord must not quarrel but be gentle*
> *to all, able to teach, patient, in humility correcting those*
> *who are in opposition, if God perhaps will grant them*
> *repentance, so that they may know the truth, and that*
> *they may come to their senses and escape the snare of the*
> *devil, having been taken captive by him to do his will.*
> *(2 Tim. 2:24-26)*

Gentleness is powerful. It usually de-escalates tension. It often
brings the other party to their senses. "A soft answer turns away
wrath" (Prov. 15:1). Regardless of the outcome, the Bible tells
us that gentleness is like clothing. It is our outward appearance.
And like the original clothing of Adam and Eve, it covers our sin.
Christians ought to be clothed with gentleness (Col. 3:12).

Gentleness acts like a shock absorber. It smooths the bumps.
Our appeals should be cushioned with gentleness and respect (1
Pet. 3:15). We should manifest the way of our Lord Jesus who is
"gentle and lowly in heart" (Matt. 11:29-30).

If you are tempted to kick someone while they're down, you
are not ready to restore. Take a deep breath. Ask the Lord to
give you a calm and tender spirit. As you enter into a difficult
conversation, take time to prepare yourself for mercy. Be clothed
with gentleness.

Checkpoint Five: Are you recognizing your own shortcomings? (Gal. 6:1)

Before confronting someone who is "overtaken in any trespass," Paul says to "[consider] yourself lest you also be tempted" (Gal. 6:1). This calls for self-awareness. Are you acknowledging that you too are a sinner? Are you searching your own heart for the same sin? Looking at yourself means to make careful observation of what's lurking inside. And if you have elements of the same sin present within you, you must deal with it before confronting your brother's sin, as Jesus taught:

> And why do you look at the speck in your brother's eye, but do not consider the plank in your own eye? Or how can you say to your brother, "Let me remove the speck from your eye"; and look, a plank is in your own eye? Hypocrite! First remove the plank from your own eye, and then you will see clearly to remove the speck from your brother's eye. (Matt. 7:3-5)

Checkpoint Six: Are you prepared to keep bearing a burden? (Gal. 6:2)

Paul calls us to "Bear one another's burdens, and so fulfill the law of Christ" (Gal. 6:2). Are you willing to bear the weight of your brother? How long are you willing to bear it? We often want quick results. We want to get everything resolved *now*! When we are in a difficult conversation that does not seem to be producing good results, patience often means that we "extend help to the brother so that he may overcome his spiritual weakness."[3] This requires patience.

Our Lord Jesus Christ has been very patient with us. How patient has He been with you? Did He require perfection of you immediately? Christ modeled such loving sacrifice on the cross as He "[bore] our griefs and carried our sorrows" (Isa. 53:4). His shouldering of man's sin is the only path to ultimate forgiveness and salvation. Before you pursue confrontation, make sure you are ready to patiently bear the weight of disappointment and to keep bearing it until the Lord chooses to relieve the burden.

Checkpoint Seven: Are you self-effacing or condescending? (Gal. 6:3)

Paul punctuates his seven-pronged heart check on confrontation with this hefty punch: "if anyone thinks himself to be something, when he is nothing, he deceives himself" (Gal. 6:3).

So here's the question: Do you think you are better and wiser than the one "overtaken in any trespass" (Gal. 6:1)? Then utterly banish this thought! A disdainfully superior attitude has no place when you confront a fallen brother. If this is your inner disposition, you need to humble yourself before acting. Prideful condescension does more harm than good.

Solomon warns young people of this:

> *There is a generation that curses its father,*
> *And does not bless its mother.*
> *There is a generation that is pure in its own eyes,*

---

3   Hendriksen, pp. 232-233.

Yet is not washed from its filthiness.
There is a generation—oh, how lofty are their eyes!
And their eyelids are lifted up.
There is a generation whose teeth are like swords,
And whose fangs are like knives,
To devour the poor from off the earth,
And the needy from among men.
(Prov. 30:11-14)

A spirit of superiority is a reconciliation killer. This is a fault practiced by young and old. If you do not conquer this destructive conversational sin when you are young, you will continue to carry it through life, and it will damage your relationships.

A Time to Speak: Pray for Courage and Clarity

Solomon aptly observed that there's "a time to keep silence, and a time to speak" (Eccl. 3:7).

Even as you should not vent petty grievances, so there are situations when we have the duty to open our mouth with the truth. We must prepare our hearts for these opportunities.

Speaking in the Public Square

While many hard conversations are best held privately behind the scenes, there are times we must speak openly in the public square.

Yet when such occasions come, we often opt for disengaged silence just like the watchmen in Isaiah: "They cannot bark; sleeping, lying down, loving to slumber" (Isa. 56:10).

This is an illustration of the harmful effects of self-indulgent watchmen. These prophets will not speak up in times of spiritual peril. They let idolatry run free. Why? Because of their laziness and refusal to bark when the intruders are infiltrating.

The Scriptures are clear—it is sometimes unloving to remain silent: "Open your mouth for the speechless, in the cause of all who are appointed to die" (Prov. 31:8).

Fear often paralyzes and keeps us from speaking as we should. "The fear of man brings a snare" (Prov. 29:25), and that snare can be shrinking silence when voicing the truth is called for. When this happens, cry out to God for courage. The Apostle Paul is a great example of this. When he was under arrest (likely in Rome), he prayed "that in [my chains] I may speak boldly, as I ought to speak" (Eph. 6:20).

We live in challenging times where key cultural gatekeepers want to suppress the truth. Simply speaking God's Word is often judged to be hate speech. Christians are losing their jobs for simply referring to males and females by their God-created biological gender, refusing to use deceptive pronouns.

The Word of God has always been an affront to rebellious mankind. Yet when Peter and John were commanded to speak no more of Jesus, they gave this bold answer: "For we cannot but speak the things which we have seen and heard" (Acts 4:20).

The prophet Jeremiah struggled with bouts of fear, but ultimately God stirred him with courage to proclaim an unpopular yet faithful message: "But His word was in my heart like a burning fire shut up in my bones; I was weary of holding it back, and I could not" (Jer. 20:9).

Having hard conversations often requires speaking hard truths. This is where hard conversations can be a blessing, for it is the truth of God alone that sets man free (John 8:31-32).

Walking in the truth is man's only hope. We ought to prepare our hearts to share that hope with clarity to others:

> *But sanctify the Lord God in your hearts, and always be ready to give a defense to everyone who asks you a reason for the hope that is in you, with meekness and fear. (1 Pet. 3:15)*

We know that our hearts can get out of kilter as we prepare for hard conversations. King David understood his vulnerability to this. He prayed that God would help him use knowledge rightly:

> *Who can understand his errors? Cleanse me from secret faults. Keep back Your servant also from presumptuous sins; let them not have dominion over me. Then I shall be blameless, and I shall be innocent of great transgression. Let the words of my mouth and the meditation of my heart be acceptable in Your sight, O LORD, my strength and my Redeemer. (Ps. 19:12-14)*

May God grant us strength to prepare our hearts in this way.

2. BE ON A MISSION TO BLESS (1 PET. 3:8-9)

When you go into battle, you must understand your mission. You must be highly focused and have a battle plan. Your objectives should be clear, your contingency plan well-ordered.

Hard conversations are a little like battles. They ought to have clearly defined objectives. Yet the goal is different. It must not be to score a victory. If you are going into the conversation to "win," you've already lost. Understanding, reconciliation, and love are the most valuable goals.

Pummeling the other party almost always jettisons godly objectives. When you engage in a difficult discussion, your assignment is to be a blessing—even when the other person has wronged you.

Finally, all of you be of one mind, having compassion for one another; love as brothers, be tenderhearted, be courteous; not returning evil for evil or reviling for reviling, but on the contrary blessing, knowing that you were called to this, that you may inherit a blessing. (1 Pet. 3:8-9)

Blessing those who revile us goes against our nature. Yet—as hard as it may be—Christ's command to "bless those who curse you" is life-giving (Luke 6:28).

God has given the "word of life" (Phil. 2:16), and we are to proclaim that word as a well of life-giving water: "The mouth of the righteous is a well of life" (Prov. 10:11).

Our speech should taste good—it should be appetizing, not bland—and it should always be adorned with grace: "Let your speech always be with grace, seasoned with salt, that you may know how you ought to answer each one" (Col. 4:6).

If we are wise, our words will promote healing and nourishment: "There is one who speaks like the piercings of a sword, but the tongue of the wise promotes health" (Prov. 12:18).

Rather than spew angry words, use your speech to build up, impart grace, and be full of kindness and tenderheartedness. Paul directs:

> Let no corrupt word proceed out of your mouth, but what is good for necessary edification, that it may impart grace to the hearers. And do not grieve the Holy Spirit of God, by whom you were sealed for the day of redemption. Let all bitterness, wrath, anger, clamor, and evil speaking be put away from you, with all malice. And be kind to one another, tenderhearted, forgiving one another, even as God in Christ forgave you. (Eph. 4:29-32)

Writing on this text, Albert Barnes distills how you can accomplish your mission to bless, even when confronting the wayward:

> Speech is an invaluable gift; a blessing of inestimable worth. We may so speak as always to do good to others. We may give them some information which they have not; impart some consolation which they need; elicit some truth by friendly discussion which we did not know before, or recall by friendly admonition those who are in danger of going astray.[4]

Let doing good be our mission in hard conversations.

---

4 Commentary on Eph. 4:29: Albert Barnes, *Notes on the Whole Bible.*

3. BE JUDICIOUS WITH YOUR WORDS: DON'T VENT EVERYTHING (PROV. 15:2)

"Get it all out!"

This is the mantra of today's psychotherapist who tells his patient to spew every grievance and leave no rotten thought unturned. But this is squarely at odds with what God's Word teaches. Paul frames the matter this way:

Let no corrupt word proceed out of your mouth, but what is good for necessary edification, that it may impart grace to the hearers. (Eph. 4:29)

Your words must be judiciously chosen to edify and impart grace; otherwise they should not be spoken.

John Gill writes:

[M]en have not a right to say what they please; good men will be cautious what they say . . . and conscious of their own weakness, they will pray to God to set a watch before their mouth, and to keep the door of their lips, and not suffer anything to come out, but that which is good for the use of edifying.[5]

A wise man is careful with his words and speaks with thoughtful restraint. Matthew Henry notes: "What we are to declare we should first consider; think twice before we speak once.[6]

---

5   John Gill, *An Exposition of the New Testament, Vol. III* (London: Matthews and Leigh, 1809), p. 96.

6   On Ecclesiastes 9: Matthew Henry, *Commentary on the Whole Bible* (1811).

The book of Proverbs drips with this vital theme:

Every prudent man acts with knowledge, but a fool lays open his folly. (Prov. 13:16)

In the multitude of words sin is not lacking, but he who restrains his lips is wise. (Prov. 10:19)

The heart of the righteous studies how to answer, but the mouth of the wicked pours forth evil. (Prov. 15:28)

The tongue of the wise uses knowledge rightly, but the mouth of fools pours forth foolishness. (Prov. 15:2)

The lips of the righteous know what is acceptable, but the mouth of the wicked what is perverse. (Prov. 10:32)

Acceptable words are wise words that are fit for the occasion. While bad speech is foolishness, becoming speech is wholesome and valuable, as the Proverbs poignantly illustrate:

A wholesome tongue is a tree of life, but perverseness in it breaks the spirit. (Prov. 15:4)

The tongue of the righteous is choice silver. (Prov. 10:20)

A word fitly spoken is like apples of gold in settings of silver. (Prov. 25:11)

Thoughtfully-delivered speech goes against the grain of knee-jerk tweets and soul-baring psychotherapy. Yet the unfiltered commentary so prevalent today is a mark of foolishness: "A fool vents all his feelings, but a wise man holds them back" (Prov. 29:11).

Charles Bridges observes:

It is sometimes thought a proof of honesty to utter all our mind. But it is rather a proof of folly. For how many things it would be far better never to speak—indeed to suppress in the very thought! How much of "foolish talking and jesting;" how many angry, detracting, uncharitable words do we utter. . . . And what wrong judgments we often pass upon men's actions, because we utter all our mind as it were in one breath, without pondering, or perhaps without materials to form a correct judgment![7]

With this truth in view, carefully study "how to answer" (Prov. 15:28), and make this psalm your prayer: "Set a guard, O LORD, over my mouth; keep watch over the door of my lips" (Ps. 141:3).

And no matter how hard your conversation is, speak words fitting for the occasion: "A man has joy by the answer of his mouth, and a word spoken in due season, how good it is!" (Prov. 15:23).

4. PREPARE TO LISTEN (JAMES 1:19)

Good communication starts with good understanding. And good understanding is impossible without careful listening. James states: "let every man be swift to hear, slow to speak" (James 1:19). God gave us one mouth and two ears for a reason!

---

7 Commentary on Proverbs 29:11: Charles Bridges, *A Commentary on Proverbs* (Edinburgh: Banner of Truth Trust, [1846] 1967), p. 567.

When we listen, we are learning. We have time to discern. Our minds are poised to sympathize rather than to respond and counter.

Our natural impulse, however, is to trumpet our own commentary rather than to thoughtfully listen. In many conversations, we are not drawing out the other person; we are simply waiting to get a word in edgewise: "Most men will proclaim each his own goodness, but who can find a faithful man?" (Prov. 20:6).

To put it plainly, listening goes against our sinful nature. David describes the wicked as "like the deaf cobra that stops its ear" (Ps. 58:4). This refusal to listen, notes John Trapp, is a "habitual, acquired, willful" deafness.[8] "A fool," Solomon affirms, "has no delight in understanding, but in expressing his own heart" (Prov. 18:2).

In contrast to our serpent-like selfishness, God intently listens to His people. "His ears are open to their cry," writes David. "The righteous cry out, and the LORD hears, and delivers them out of all their troubles" (Ps. 34:15, 17).

What a blessing this is—a God who hears our pleas!

Listening is one way we serve one another (Mark 10:43-45). It's how we get on the same wavelength with another person.

Some women actually struggle to hear men's voices. They have what is called "cookie-bite hearing loss." They can hear high and low frequencies but not mid-range sounds, where men's voices often register.[9]

---

8 Commentary on Psalm 58:4: John Trapp, *Complete Commentary on the Bible*.

9 Lise Ragbir, "I have a hard time hearing men talk," Salon, May 21, 2022. Accessed

While this is a rare condition, we all have a natural tendency to only listen to one wavelength. We selfishly tune others out and don't really focus on what they're saying.

Listening to get on the other person's wavelength is critical if we ever hope to have true understanding. Good communication necessitates careful listening. This only happens when we listen long enough to hear a person's full mind. This takes self-control.

Listening requires humility. Lending a humble ear helps us get past preconceived notions that are often wrong because, in our pride, we've failed to hear the other person's side of a matter. "The first one to plead his cause seems right, until his neighbor comes and examines him" (Prov. 18:17).

Rather than jump to hasty conclusions, we need to carefully listen to the other person's views and truly hear their heart. To do this we must hold our tongue, suppress our racing thoughts, and really tune in to them, "He who has knowledge spares his words, and a man of understanding is of a calm spirit" (Prov. 17:27).

Eliminate Distractions

To listen as we ought, we must eliminate distractions!

Multitasking is a conversation killer. So put your phone away. Stop picking it up! Put it out of sight. It destroys respect. It causes misunderstanding. It tells everyone you are not concentrating on them. You've bailed out on the conversation. You've dishonored the other person.

July 3, 2023, https://www.salon.com/2022/05/21/i-have-a-hard-time-hearing-men-talk-literally-thats-not-the-most-troubling-part-of-my-diagnosis/.

So as you prepare to listen, make this your heart: "Let each of you look out not only for his own interests, but also for the interests of others" (Phil. 2:4).

5. DON'T INTERRUPT (PROV. 18:13)

Interrupting is the bane of good communication.

We are often so intent on answering that we don't bother to listen. We rudely interrupt and fire back, not letting the other person finish their thought. While a healthy back-and-forth can be helpful to get to the bottom of things, interrupting someone mid-sentence is a conversation killer.

Scripture denounces this practice in no uncertain terms: "He who answers a matter before he hears it, it is folly and shame to him" (Prov. 18:13).

James also lowers the boom against such antics: "If anyone among you thinks he is religious, and does not bridle his tongue . . . this one's religion is useless" (James 1:26). The contrast he gives is stark, but instructive: where "strife is, there is confusion and every evil work. But the wisdom that is from above is first pure, then peaceable, gentle, and easy to be entreated" (James 3:16-17 KJV).

How "easy to be entreated" are you?

Consider these sobering proverbs:

Do you see a man hasty in his words? There is more hope for a fool than for him. (Prov. 29:20)

Whoever has no rule over his own spirit is like a city broken down, without walls. (Prov. 25:28)

We need to stop making excuses and get our mouths under control. Guarding our tongues is a must.

> *Whoever guards his mouth and tongue keeps his soul from troubles. (Prov. 21:23)*

> *He who guards his mouth preserves his life, but he who opens wide his lips shall have destruction. (Prov. 13:3)*

Listen carefully. Stop interrupting!

Show respect for the other person and let them fully relate their mind.

6. ASK QUESTIONS (PROV. 20:5)

Even as careful listening is vital to good communication, so are thoughtfully-placed questions.

Solomon writes, "Counsel in the heart of man is like deep water, but a man of understanding will draw it out" (Prov. 20:5).

Drawing out the other person through respectful questions shows that we care to know their mind. This is crucial, particularly in the husband-wife relationship. Peter calls on husbands to dwell with their wives "with understanding" (1 Pet. 3:7). A husband can only accomplish this by knowing what his bride is thinking. The best action he can take to know her better is to ask questions. This is one of our best communication tools in the conversational toolbox.

This is true of every relationship. By asking questions, we better understand one another.

It is a blessing to others when we delight to understand them. On the other hand, it is a discouragement when we selfishly show we don't care what they are thinking.

Remember this convicting proverb: "A fool has no delight in understanding, but in expressing his own heart" (Prov. 18:2).

With this in view, focus on drawing out the thoughts of others rather than selfishly expressing yourself. Here are some basic questions that will help you understand a person better:

> *"What do you mean by that?"*
> *"Tell me more."*
> *"Can you help me see that more clearly?"*
> *"Can you give me an example of that?"*
> *"I'm slow; can you say it a different way?"*
> *"One more time, help me get this right!"*

The conversation that Job had with his friends is instructive. It was a tough discussion. Both parties veered off the path of good communication. In commenting on the scene, Matthew Henry notes: "Every one feels most from his own burden; few feel from other people's."[10]

The best way to feel other people's burdens is to ask questions!

Learn How to Throw the Ball

Many years ago I heard of a way to help couples govern their conversations when they are having a hard time listening to each other. Here it is:

---

10 On Job 6:1-7: Matthew Henry, *Commentary on the Whole Bible* (1811).

Get a tennis ball. Have one spouse hold the ball. As long as she is holding the ball, she has the floor. When she is done talking, she asks the listener a simple question, "Now, tell me what I just said."

She will not give the ball to the listener until the listener repeats her message accurately. This governs the back-and-forth of a couple who is having a hard time hearing one another, always interrupting one another, etc.

7. MONITOR YOUR TONE (1 TIM. 4:16)

Speaking with a bad tone is another one of the biggest conversation killers. Tone matters; it's not neutral! Researchers say that tone communicates even more than words—so watch out. Watch your tone! Heighten self-awareness in *how* you communicate.

Paul writes to Timothy, "Take heed to yourself and to the doctrine. Continue in them, for in doing this you will save both yourself and those who hear you" (1 Tim. 4:16).

It is not just what we say but how we say it that directs the course of conversations. So pay attention to tone! Be self-conscious about how you come across when you are talking through difficult matters.

Tone communicates more powerfully than words. A respectful tone can diffuse a controversy while an angry tone can further inflame it.

Solomon writes, "A soft answer turns away wrath, but a harsh word stirs up anger" (Prov. 15:1).

How we speak is thus essential. "The tongue of the wise uses knowledge rightly, but the mouth of fools pours forth foolishness" (Prov. 15:2).

On the negative side, your tone can be:

- Angry
- Pompous
- Cutting
- Condescending
- Belittling
- Harsh
- Dismissive
- Irritated
- Rushed

In contrast to these vices, your tone should be seasoned with grace and governed by love: "Love does not parade itself, is not puffed up; does not behave rudely" (1 Cor. 13:4-5).

Our tone should also drip with the grace of God: "Let your speech always be with grace, seasoned with salt, that you may know how you ought to answer each one" (Col. 4:6). So monitor your tone and reflect Christ in how you speak to others!

8. CONTROL YOUR BODY LANGUAGE (ECCL. 8:1)

When it comes to conversations, much is communicated through our body language.

What people see on our faces will tend to be reflected back to us in kind. In most situations, we are responders. We react to the body language of others. And our body language easily sets others off. Just as "grievous words stir up anger" (Prov. 15:1 KJV), so does an "angry countenance" (Prov. 25:23).

We should thus work to control our body language. Yet our main reason for doing so should not be to pragmatically seek a better outcome. No, we should control ourselves under the power of the Holy Spirit in order to humbly honor God and show genuine care for our fellow man.

Paul told the Corinthian church, "glorify God in your body" (1 Cor. 6:20), so what we do with our body when we talk to others should glorify Him.

The bottom line: We're not free to use any body language we please. Not only are an angry countenance, the waving of the arms, and a scowl on the face harmful mannerisms that torpedo healthy conversations, but they reveal a serious heart problem that must be addressed.

Pride drives selfish body language like nothing else. Thinking more highly of ourselves than we ought (Rom. 12:3) directly affects our physical behavior; it showcases our prideful heart in our gestures. Scripture is replete with such examples.

Children who rebel against their parents show the condition of their heart by their haughty eyes: "There is a generation— oh, how lofty are their eyes! And their eyelids are lifted up" (Prov. 30:11, 13).

An evil man, in similar fashion, "winks with his eyes, he shuffles his feet, he points with his fingers" (Prov. 6:13). He "[refuses] to heed" and shrugs his shoulders (Zech. 7:11).

He shows arrogance through his mouth and tongue: "Against whom do you make a wide mouth and stick out the tongue? Are you not children of transgression, offspring of falsehood?" (Isa. 57:4). Those who mocked Jerusalem's fall in Jeremiah's time likewise vaunted their disdain:

> *All who pass by clap their hands at you; they hiss and shake their heads at the daughter of Jerusalem: "Is this the city that is called 'The perfection of beauty, the joy of the whole earth'?" All your enemies have opened their mouth against you; they hiss and gnash their teeth. (Lam. 2:15-16)*

The prideful body language of those who would mock Christ when He went to the cross is vividly revealed here: "All those who see Me ridicule Me; they shoot out the lip, they shake the head" (Ps. 22:7).

This bad body language was fulfilled—just as prophesied:

> *And those who passed by blasphemed Him, wagging their heads and saying, "You who destroy the temple and build it in three days, save Yourself! If You are the Son of God, come down from the cross." (Matt. 27:39-40)*

These are all examples of "a proud look" which God says He "hates" as an "abomination" (Prov. 6:16-17).

Proverbs sheds further light on the matter: "A proud and haughty man—'Scoffer' is his name; he acts with arrogant pride" (Prov. 21:24). The Hebrew word translated "scoffer" means to "make mouths at, talk arrogantly."[11] So a scoffer (also translated "scorner")—by definition—shows bad body language that flows from a prideful heart.

---

11 *lûwts* (H3887) in James Strong, *The Exhaustive Concordance of the Bible* (1890).

Such body language should have no place in our conversations. A wise man, states Solomon, puts off such pride and shows humility in his demeanor.

> *Who is like a wise man? . . . A man's wisdom makes his face shine, and the sternness of his face is changed. (Eccl. 8:1)*

Commenting on this verse, Keil and Delitzsch describe this drastic transformation in body language:

> *Wisdom gives bright eyes to a man, a gentle countenance, a noble expression; it refines and dignifies his external appearance and his demeanour; the hitherto rude external, and the regardless, selfish, and bold deportment, are changed.*[12]

We should "talk no more so very proudly" (1 Sam. 2:3) but rather "be clothed with humility" (1 Pet. 5:5), and this should manifest itself in our body language. Paul gives this helpful direction: "Present your bodies as a living sacrifice" (Rom. 12:1-2).

When we love our neighbor as ourselves (Matt. 22:39), we will treat them as we would want to be treated. We will be motivated by humble sacrifice, not self-exaltation. And this should show itself in our every gesture.

Your countenance should also reflect a desire for peace and reconciliation (James 3:18). Smile! Maintain good eye contact. Humbly show respect for the other person, and leave the results in the hands of God.

---

12 Commentary on Eccl. 8:1: C.F. Keil & F. Delitzsch, *Commentary on the Old Testament, Vol. 6* (Peabody, MA: Hendrickson Publishers, [1866-91] 2006), p. 742.

9. DON'T COMPARE (PROV. 25:27)

Left to our sinful self, we talk like we're the center of the universe.

When we hear another person tell their story, we immediately connect it to our story. "Yes, the same thing happened to me; let me tell you about it . . ." The conversation is diverted to focus on our experience rather than theirs. As comparing begins, listening ends.

This serious problem reveals an underlying sin pattern—self-centeredness. The word narcissism describes it well. This word was coined from the Greek myth of Narcissus who, according to legend, fell in love with his own reflection in the waters of a pool.[13]

The Bible tells us how ridiculous this is: "to seek one's own glory is not glory," Solomon declared (Prov. 25:27). For men "to set forth their own excellencies . . . is not glorious and praiseworthy, but dishonourable," John Gill adds.[14]

Yet self-admiration keeps us focused on ourselves. We would rather hear about ourselves than learn about others. This is a fool's posture: "A fool has no delight in understanding, but in expressing his own heart" (Prov. 18:2).

To correct this error, we need to embrace humility by genuinely caring to learn about other people and not shifting conversations back to our personal story: "in lowliness of mind let each esteem

---

13 Online Etymology Dictionary, "*narcissism* (n.)," Accessed June 23, 2023, https://www.etymonline.com/search?q=narcissism.

14 Commentary on Prov. 25:27: John Gill, *An Exposition of the Old Testament, Vol. IV* (London: Matthews and Leigh, 1810), p. 504.

other better than themselves. Look not every man on his own things, but every man also on the things of others" (Phil. 2:3).

So stop comparing and truly listen!

10. DON'T HARP (PROV. 17:9)

Don't harp when you have hard conversations!

We all know what "harping" is—it is repetition of the same old thing. It can include repeating your point over and over again. It can involve rehearsing old offenses. "You've told me that fifty times!" you hear in response.

It's when you're "like a broken record," where the needle can't advance due to a scratch on the vinyl, so it keeps repeating the same line over and over. It's like hitting replay, replay, replay on a video clip.

How do you cure it?

First realize that these "vain repetitions" are driven by self-love rather than true love for the other person: "Love suffers long and is kind; . . . [it] bears all things" (1 Cor. 13:4, 7). Love doesn't harbor grudges. Love moves on for the good of the other person. "He who covers a transgression seeks love, but he who repeats a matter separates friends" (Prov. 17:9).

With this understood, resolve to stop repeating yourself. This may not happen overnight because harping is habit-forming. It can become an entrenched pattern in our younger years that is hard to break. Unless we get serious about the problem, we will keep falling into the same ditch as we age. But if we are going to act like Christians, we need to repent and end this bad practice.

It's time to love your neighbor enough to stop harping at them!

II. DON'T USE INFLAMMATORY DEFAULT EXPRESSIONS (PROV. 17:14)

Beware of reliance on inflammatory default expressions.

In other words, don't throw gas on a fire.

Phrases such as "Come on," "Give me a break," "Are you serious?" "What!!!???" and "Stop yelling at me!" can explode a conversation almost instantly.

James writes: "See how great a forest a little fire kindles! And the tongue is a fire, a world of iniquity" (James 3:5-6).

Solomon uses water trickling from a small breach in a dam to make the same point: "The beginning of strife is like releasing water" (Prov. 17:14).

Adam Clarke elaborates on this metaphor:

> As soon as the smallest breach is made in the dike or dam, the water begins to press from all parts towards the breach; the resistance becomes too great to be successfully opposed, so that dikes and all are speedily swept away. Such is the beginning of contentions.[15]

Even as Solomon paints this scary image of the fallout of ill-placed words, he also gives the antidote: "The beginning of strife is like releasing water; therefore stop contention before a quarrel starts" (Prov. 17:14).

---

15 On Prov. 17:13: Adam Clarke, *Commentary on the Whole Bible* (1831).

The key to this is to stop using incendiary default expressions that will only aggravate. Note that a "wholesome tongue is a tree of life, but perverseness in it breaks the spirit" (Prov. 15:4).

So let's lay aside our spiteful pet phrases and use "sound speech that cannot be condemned" (Titus 2:8)!

12. DON'T PROJECT OUTCOMES (PROV. 3:5-6)

Beware of projecting outcomes when you are headed for a hard conversation.

We often wrongly think that, if we have an honest discussion, we will lose a relationship. When we are dealing with an offended party, we put them in a box and say, "I'm not going to talk to him because he never listens anyway." We think, "If I say this, he will do nothing about it."

We act as if we're omniscient. We think we *know* how things are going to turn out.

The truth is, we don't know outcomes—only God does—and we should pursue hard conversations when it's our obligation to do so. If we achieve good understanding and are reconciled with an offended brother or sister, praise the Lord! But if not, we have done the right thing. We must simply do our duty and trust God with the results.

Trust in the LORD with all your heart, and lean not on your own understanding; in all your ways acknowledge Him, and He shall direct your paths. (Prov. 3:5-6)

13. FOCUS ON THE BEST BIBLICAL OBJECTIVES (MATT. 6:33)

While we cannot dictate outcomes, we should always aim for the very best biblical objectives.

Know where you want to go in your conversation, and then focus on that end. This is not manipulation when your goals are biblical goals, humbly pursued before God. Rather, it is prayerful intention. Wise people establish in their minds the best possible outcome. Everything they do serves that outcome. It helps if both parties can agree on what the best outcome is and then make it a shared aim.

This is vital in marriage. If you are husband and wife, then you are to view each other as "one flesh" (Gen. 2:24). You should strive to deepen your unity, not break it up. You should be going, together, in the best possible direction.

Here are some key biblical outcomes to strive toward.

Obey the Word of God

The psalms declare that God's Word is "a lamp to my feet and a light to my path" (Ps. 119:105).

His Word is not just one helpful lamp; it's the only source of unshakable truth there is—for, "There is no wisdom or understanding or counsel against the LORD" (Prov. 21:30).

The truth of God's Word therefore should be the beginning and end of any hard discussion. It should frame every point and guide every outcome. It should reign as paramount.

If you are appealing to another Christian, this should be the shared starting point to work through every difficulty. If you're dialoguing with a non-Christian, know that the proclamation of God's Word will not return void even if every other objective you're aiming for fails (Isa. 55:11). That God's Word was reverently upheld is an outcome worth the effort.

Glorify God

Self-glory is at the heart of ten thousand woes. When we seek God's glory alone, wrongs are righted, wounds are healed, and lives are restored.

So let this outcome drive our discussions: "Not unto us, O LORD, not unto us, but to Your name give glory, because of Your mercy, because of Your truth" (Ps. 115:1).

Renounce Pride and Embrace Humility

Pride destroys while humility rescues.

The Scripture is clear:

> [T]he LORD [will] cut off . . . the tongue that speaks proud things. (Ps. 12:3)

> Before destruction the heart of a man is haughty, and before honor is humility. (Prov. 18:12)

So renounce pride and embrace humility. This should be a priority.

> . . . be clothed with humility, for "God resists the proud, but gives grace to the humble." Therefore humble yourselves under the mighty hand of God, that He may exalt you in

due time, casting all your care upon Him, for He cares for you. (1 Pet. 5:5-7)

Set Aside Petty Grievances for the Greater Good

Paul tells us that love "is not easily provoked" (1 Cor. 13:5 KJV), and Solomon adds, "The discretion of a man makes him slow to anger, and his glory is to overlook a transgression" (Prov. 19:11).

So set aside petty grievances for the greater good of your relationship!

Forgive One Another

Unforgiveness is a blight that devastates relationships.

As Christians, we've been forgiven much by God, so we should freely forgive others: "if anyone has a complaint against another; even as Christ forgave you, so you also must do" (Col. 3:13).

Seek Reconciliation

Rather than sulk and stew when wronged, we should seek reconciliation: "Moreover if your brother sins against you, go and tell him his fault between you and him alone. If he hears you, you have gained your brother" (Matt. 18:15).

Even when attempts to reconcile fail, reconciliation is a biblical outcome worth pursuing.

Forsake Sin and Clean House

When we become complacent and passive, sin can easily creep into our homes and families and gain a deadly foothold.

This happened to Jacob's family for a season before he took charge and cleaned house: "And Jacob said to his household and to all who were with him, 'Put away the foreign gods that are among you, purify yourselves, and change your garments'" (Gen. 35:2).

There are times when we must make a break with sin and clean house. It may involve hard discussions with close family members, but it's an outcome we must tackle with humble repentance.

Restore a Brother Overtaken in a Fault

When a brother stumbles, we should humbly seek to restore him:

> *Brethren, if a man is overtaken in any trespass, you who are spiritual restore such a one in a spirit of gentleness, considering yourself lest you also be tempted. Bear one another's burdens, and so fulfill the law of Christ. (Gal. 6:1-2)*

This is a worthy outcome when it is pursued in the fear of God.

Seek True Repentance

Repentance is more than an expression of guilty sorrow. It is a turning away from sin and a turning toward God:

> *For godly sorrow produces repentance leading to salvation, not to be regretted; but the sorrow of the world produces death. For observe this very thing, that you sorrowed in a godly manner: What diligence it produced in you, what clearing of yourselves, what indignation, what fear, what vehement*

> *desire, what zeal, what vindication! In all things you proved*
> *yourselves to be clear in this matter. (2 Cor. 7:10-11)*

Seeking true repentance in our hearts and in the heart of our brother is a goal we should pursue.

Warn of False Teachers and Teaching

False teachers are a serious danger we should warn others against.

Note the love and care of the Apostle John: "These things I have written to you concerning those who try to deceive you" (1 John 2:26).

Rescuing unsuspecting brothers from false teaching and teachers is an outcome that deserves our careful focus.

Spur One Another to Love and Good Works

When we see a brother or sister who has been lulled to sleep or who has lost their first love for God, we should spur them on to faithful living: "And let us consider one another to provoke unto love and to good works" (Heb. 10:24 KJV).

Walk in Love

At every turn and challenge in our relationships, we should walk in love:

> *Therefore be imitators of God as dear children. And walk*
> *in love, as Christ also has loved us and given Himself for*
> *us, an offering and a sacrifice to God for a sweet-smelling*
> *aroma. (Eph. 5:1-2)*

This should drive every outcome as we engage in hard discussions.

Seek First Christ's Kingdom and Righteousness

Above all things, we should "seek first the kingdom of God and His righteousness" (Matt. 6:33). When we set this as our chief outcome, our eyes will look upward, and we will gain an eternal perspective.

Even when relationships go awry or remain in limbo, we can rejoice that God is exalted and His ways championed.

This is the end we should pursue in every relationship challenge we face.

"Look, and look again unto Jesus."

To Him be all the glory and praise!

CONCLUSION

Learning how to talk is a lifelong challenge. I know this to be true from personal experience. Over the course of my life, I have personally shown a lack of wisdom in the use of my tongue and have committed every one of the sins outlined in this book.

A few days before completing this work, I read these words from Matthew Henry, which I found to be convicting: "Those that speak too much seldom think they have said enough; and, when the mouth is opened in passion, the ear is shut to reason."[1]

Yet there's good news: though our tongues are prone to wander, we have an unswerving "rudder" to guide us!

If we believe God is sovereign, then we must believe that the difficult conversations that come our way are from Him—and they are for our good, for God causes all things to work for good for those who are the called according to His purpose (Rom. 8:28).

We are in good hands! If we seek His wisdom for help, God will faithfully lead us through the hard conversations we face

---

1   On Job 19:1-5: Matthew Henry, *Commentary on the Whole Bible* (1811).

(James 1:5). By His grace, He will teach us how to talk as we ought, again and again.

When we find ourselves engaging in *controversial subjects, pivotal relationships, strong opinions, where important outcomes are at play,* we can know that it is God who has drawn us into them for our good and the good of others—and that He will give us the words to speak. As we purpose "that [our] mouth shall not transgress" (Ps. 17:3), He will faithfully lead us.

"Look, and look again unto Jesus!"

With His divine help, our speech can "always [be] with grace, seasoned with salt, that [we] may know how [we] ought to answer each one" (Col. 4:6).

SCRIPTURE INDEX

12:36 16
15:19 11
18:15 30,60
22:39 21,53
27:39-40 52

Mark
10:43-45 44

Luke
6:28 39

John
7:46 17
8:31-32 38

Acts
4:20 37

Romans
7:23 15
8:6 32
8:28 65
8:29 17
12:1 13
12:1-2.................................... 53
12:3 51

1 Corinthians
6:20 13,51
13:1 21
13:4-5.................................... 50
13:4, 7 55
13:4-8.................................... 28
13:5 29,51,60

2 Corinthians
3:18 17
7:10-11 62
10:5 14

Galatians
5:19-21 11
5:22-26 32
5:23 33
6:1 31-35
6:1-2..................................... 61
6:1-3..................................... 30
6:2 34
6:3 35

Ephesians
3:17 28
4:15 28
4:17 15